Flavour

YORKS

RECIPES

Compiled by Julia Skinner

THE FRANCIS FRITH COLLECTION

www.francisfrith.com

First published in the United Kingdom in 2010 by The Francis Frith Collection®

This edition published exclusively for Identity Books in 2010 ISBN 978-1-84589-540-2
Reprinted in 2011

British Library Cataloguing in Publication Data

Flavours of... Yorkshire
Compiled by Julia Skinner

The Francis Frith Collection
Unit 6, Oakley Business Park,
Wylye Road, Dinton,
Wiltshire SP3 5EU
Tel: +44 (0) 1722 716 376
Email: info@francisfrith.co.uk
www.francisfrith.com

Printed and bound in England

Front Cover: **YORK, GOODRAMGATE 1892** 30631p
Frontispiece: **BOLTON ABBEY, COUPLE BY THE ABBEY c1886** 18510x

The colour-tinting is for illustrative purposes only, and is not intended to be historically accurate

CONTENTS

HULL, ST ANDREW'S DOCK c1955 HI33037

RECIPE

NORTH SEA FISHERMAN'S PIE

Yorkshire fishermen have ventured out for centuries from small villages such as Runswick Bay, larger harbours such as Bridlington, Scarborough and Whitby, and the great port and fishing centre of Hull, which was once the home of the world's largest deep-water fishing fleet. Hull trawlers fished the North Sea, the White Sea, and the fringes of the Arctic, particularly for cod. In former years a fish pie was the traditional dish to be eaten in Yorkshire at Easter, on Good Friday.

<u>For the filling:</u>
350ml/12 fl oz milk
1 bay leaf
Half an onion, finely sliced
450g/1 lb haddock or cod fillet
225g/8oz smoked haddock fillet
3 hard-boiled eggs, chopped
25g/1oz butter or margarine
25g/1oz plain flour
75g/3oz shelled prawns
2 tablespoonfuls chopped fresh
   parsley
Lemon juice to taste

<u>For the topping:</u>
500g /1¼ lbs potatoes, cooked
40g/1½ oz butter
60ml/ 4 tablespoonfuls milk
115g/4oz grated hard cheese
   of choice
Salt and pepper

Place the milk, the bay leaf and sliced onion in a saucepan over a medium heat and add the fish. Cover, and poach the fish lightly for 10 minutes. Strain, discard the bay leaf and reserve the milk for the sauce. Flake the fish into a buttered pie dish, discarding the skin and any remaining bones. Add the chopped eggs to the fish.

Melt 25g/1oz butter in a saucepan on a low heat, stir in the flour and cook gently for 1 minute, stirring continually. Remove the pan from the heat and stir in the reserved milk that the fish was poached in, a little at a time and stirring continually so that no lumps are formed. When all the milk has been mixed in, return the pan to the heat and bring the mixture to the boil, stirring continually as the sauce thickens, then simmer the sauce for about 4 minutes, still stirring all the time. Remove from the heat and stir in the prawns.

Add the parsley, lemon juice and seasoning to taste. Pour the sauce over the fish and eggs in the pie dish, and gently mix it all together.

Pre-heat the oven to 180°C/350°F/Gas Mark 4.

<u>To make the topping</u>

Gently heat 40g/1½ oz butter in 60ml/ 4 tablespoonfuls of milk in a small saucepan until the butter melts, then add the milk and melted butter to the cooked potatoes, mash and then beat until smooth. Spoon over the fish pie mixture to cover, then score the surface with a fork. Sprinkle the grated cheese over the pie before baking. Bake the pie in the pre-heated oven for 25-30 minutes, until the top is golden.

SCARBOROUGH, THE PIERHEAD
1890 23472

RECIPE

HERRINGS IN OATMEAL

Herrings were a particularly important catch for fishermen along Yorkshire's coastline in the 19th century. Herrings, known to fishermen as the 'silver darlings', are particularly nutritious and were sought after as a staple part of the diet in Victorian times. This recipe serves them with a coating of oatmeal, also a staple part of the diet in Yorkshire in the past.

4 herrings
50g/2oz medium oatmeal
Half a teaspoonful of salt
25-50g/1-2oz butter
Juice of half a lemon
Chopped fresh parsley

Clean and bone the herrings, and dry them. Mix the salt in with the oatmeal, and use this to coat the herrings on both sides, pressing the oatmeal well into the fish.

Melt the butter in a large frying pan and fry the herrings for about 3 minutes on each side, adding more butter as necessary. Place the cooked fish on a hot dish and keep warm.

Add a little more butter to the pan, and when it is melted and frothy add the lemon juice, warm it through and then pour the sauce over the fish. Sprinkle with chopped fresh parsley and serve.

FACT BOX

During the 19th and early 20th centuries the attractive coastal village of Staithes was a fishing port of some standing, as Whitby-built yawls and cobles ventured out in pairs to catch haddock, cod and mackerel. A coble (pronounced 'cobble') is a very ancient type of fishing boat found in Yorkshire that goes back to Viking times. It is clinker built, with a flat bottom for landing on the beach. Photograph S176001 (below) shows fish wives and old men at Staithes c1900, baiting the lines for the fishermen with mussels or limpets. The women are wearing traditional 'Staithes bonnets', which were flared at the sides to stop the coils of hooks and lines becoming entangled in their hair. Initially white in colour, if a woman was widowed the colour of her bonnet was changed to black, worn for some time after the bereavement, and then exchanged for one of a mauve coloured material. Women in Staithes were still wearing these bonnets right up until the 1960s.

STAITHES, BAITING THE LINES c1900 S176001

RECIPE

STUFFED MACKEREL WITH GOOSEBERRY SAUCE

Gooseberries have long been a favourite accompaniment to mackerel in English cookery, and this sauce is particularly appropriate for Yorkshire-caught mackerel since the town of Egton Bridge on the North Yorkshire Moors inland from Whitby is known for its annual gooseberry show, held in August, where gardeners compete to see who has grown the largest or tastiest gooseberries. It is the oldest gooseberry show in the country, having been established in 1800. The 2009 show saw local man Bryan Nellist take the prize for the heaviest gooseberry ever grown in the UK, a feat later recognised as a world record. His Woodpecker berry weighed 2.19oz (62.0 grams), beating the previous 16-year record set by Kelvin Archer from Cheshire.

> 4 mackerel, gutted and de-scaled
> 1 tablespoonful chopped parsley
> 1 tablespoonful chopped thyme
> Half a teaspoonful grated lemon rind
> 1 tablespoonful lemon juice
> 25g/1oz soft white breadcrumbs
> Seasoned flour
> 225g/8oz gooseberries
> Sugar to taste
> A little butter or oil

Wash and dry the mackerel and clean them. Mix the parsley, thyme, lemon rind, lemon juice and soft breadcrumbs and stuff the mackerel with this mixture. Roll the fish lightly in seasoned flour. Melt a little butter or oil in a baking pan and, when it is very hot, put in the mackerel. Put into the oven and bake at 180°C/350° F/Gas Mark 4 for 25 minutes, carefully turning the fish over halfway through.

Meanwhile, for the gooseberry sauce, simmer the gooseberries in a very little water until they are soft. Rub them through a sieve and sweeten lightly, with the sugar, to taste.

Warm the gooseberry sauce through before serving with the mackerel.

WHITBY, THE PEART CHILDREN 1891 28866

RECIPE

BUTTERED CRAB

The excellent shellfish, lobster and crab caught along Yorkshire's coastline is sought after by restaurants throughout the north of England.

> 450g/1 lb fresh or frozen crab meat
> 2 anchovy fillets
> 150ml/5 fl oz dry white wine
> A pinch of grated nutmeg or mace
> 4 tablespoonfuls fresh white breadcrumbs
> Salt and freshly ground black pepper
> 75g/3oz butter

Flake the crab meat coarsely. Pound up the anchovies in the wine, and add the nutmeg, breadcrumbs and seasonings. Put into a saucepan and bring gently to the boil, then simmer for 3 minutes. Mix the flaked crab meat with the butter and add to the hot wine mixture, stir and cook gently for 4 minutes.

Serve the buttered crab with slices or fingers of hot buttered toast.

SCARBOROUGH, FISH MARKET c1955 S71131

R. REWCROFT.
FISHERMAN.
WE SELL
OUR OWN CATCH.

F. D.
FISH

CRABS
LOBSTE

MAINPRIZE.
ISHERMAN.
S & LOBSTERS.
OWN CATCH.

W.E PROSSER
SHELL FISH MERCHANT
Dressed Crabs
a Speciality

JAC

KIPPERS
POSTED.
4-5- PER
BOX
POST PAID

KIPPERS
OAK SMOKED
KIPPERS
4-5- A Box
POST PAID

KIPPERS

CRABS

Flavours of ...
YORKSHIRE
FISH AND SHELLFISH

BRIDLINGTON, SS YORKSHIREMAN 1932 B206179

THE SHAMBLES

Photograph 61722x (below) shows the historic Shambles of the city of York. The word 'shambles' comes from the Old English 'shamel', which means a bench or a stall, and in medieval York this was the area where the butchers prepared and sold meat from such 'shambles'. Those wide shelves for displaying meat can be seen at the front of the shops in this photograph, and these and the hooks overhead indicate that even in the early years of the 20th century this was still the traditional part of the city for butchers' shops. The narrowness of the street kept the shops cool in the days before refrigeration, and prevented direct sunlight from reaching the meat.

YORK, CHILDREN IN THE SHAMBLES 1909 61722x

RECIPE

BARNSLEY CHOPS WITH PORT AND REDCURRANT SAUCE

The moors and dales of Yorkshire are grazed by sheep, which for centuries provided the raw material for the county's important textile industry. However, sheep have also played a part in Yorkshire's food history – it was sheep's milk which was used by the monks of Jervaulx Abbey in the Middle Ages to produce the first Wensleydale cheese, and a special cut for a lamb chop is named after the Yorkshire town of Barnsley, which is believed to have originated from the Brooklands Hotel in the town – a Barnsley chop is cut from the centre of the loin across both chops, producing a butterfly shape. In this recipe, the delicious, easy-to-make sauce accompanies the beautiful flavour of Yorkshire-reared lamb beautifully. This quantity makes enough sauce for 4 people, so increase the amount if you are feeding more. If Barnsley chops prove hard to find, lamb loin chops can be used instead, allowing 2 per person.

> Allow 1 Barnsley lamb chop per person
> (or 2 lamb loin chops per person)
> A little oil for brushing the chops
> Salt and pepper to taste
> 4 tablespoonfuls of redcurrant jelly
> 1 wine glass of port

Melt the redcurrant jelly in a small saucepan, then add the port and bring to the boil. Allow to boil for about 5 minutes to reduce down and thicken slightly, then turn the heat to low and keep the sauce warm whilst you cook the chops.

Season the chops with salt and pepper, then either fry in a little oil or brush them with a little oil and place them under a pre-heated grill and cook for about 8-10 minutes, or less if you like your lamb very pink, turning the chops over half way through the cooking time. They should be well browned on the outside, but slightly pink in the middle.

Serve the chops piping hot, accompanied with the sauce.

BARNSLEY, MARKET HILL 1948 B333004

RECIPE

POOR MAN'S GOOSE

In many parts of Yorkshire it was the custom in the past to eat roast goose on Christmas Day, and then to make Goose Pies on St Stephen's Day (better known now as Boxing Day, 26th December) and give some to needier neighbours who could not afford to make their own. Those who were not lucky recipients of Goose Pies could always make do with this cheaper alternative dish, which was not actually made from goose but from ox liver.

> 450g/1 lb ox liver
> Seasoned flour
> A small amount of oil or fat for frying
> 3 onions, sliced
> 1 tablespoonful chopped sage
> 300ml/ ½ pint stock
> 450g/1 lb potatoes
> A small knob of butter

Pre-heat the oven to 180°C/350°F/Gas Mark 4.

Slice the liver into thin strips and coat them in the seasoned flour. Fry the sliced onions in the oil or fat until they are soft, then add the liver and fry lightly for 2 minutes. Put the liver and onions into an ovenproof dish, sprinkle over the chopped sage, and then pour over the stock. Peel the potatoes and cut them into thin slices. Arrange the potato slices on top of the liver and onions. Cover the dish with a lid or foil, and bake in the pre-heated oven for 1 hour. Remove the lid or foil for the last 20 minutes of the cooking time, and brush the potatoes with melted butter to make them brown and crisp at the edges.

RECIPE

WAKEFIELD RABBIT

4 rabbit joints
Seasoned flour
1 egg, beaten
50g/2oz dried breadcrumbs
1 level teaspoonful mixed dried herbs
  - thyme, marjoram and parsley
A pinch of cayenne pepper, to taste
Salt
25g/1oz butter

Pre-heat the oven to 180°C/350°F/Gas Mark 4.

Toss the rabbit joints in the seasoned flour, coating all sides.
Mix the breadcrumbs with the herbs, salt and pepper and
cayenne pepper. Dip each rabbit joint in the beaten egg,
and then coat it with the herby breadcrumb mixture.

Put the rabbit joints in a roasting tin, and dot the top of
each joint with small pieces of butter. Roast the joints in the
pre-heated oven for about 1½ hours, or until the joints have
a crispy finish.

RECIPE

WENSLEYDALE TARTS

These savoury tarts are delicious warm or cold, and make an ideal first course or a supper dish, or to take on a picnic. This quantity makes 6 small individual tarts, but if preferred you can just make one large tart instead, using a dish or tin 22-24cm (9-10 inches) in diameter.

> 225g/8oz shortcrust pastry
> 225g/8oz onions, finely chopped
> 150ml/ ¼ pint milk
> 115g/4oz Wensleydale cheese, grated
> 50g/2oz butter or margarine
> 25g/1oz plain flour
> 15g / ½ oz fresh breadcrumbs
> A good pinch of freshly grated nutmeg
> Salt and freshly ground black pepper

Pre-heat the oven to 200°C/400°F/Gas Mark 6 and place a baking tray in the oven to heat up. Grease either 6 small tart or patty tins about 9cm (3½ inches) in diameter or one large tart tin 22-24cm (9-10 inches) in diameter.

Roll out the pastry on a lightly floured surface, and use it to line the prepared tart tins. Prick the pastry bases with a fork, then line the base of each tin with a piece of greaseproof paper, fill with baking beans and 'bake blind' in the pre-heated oven for 15 minutes, standing the tins on the hot baking tray in the oven (this helps the pastry bases to cook through). When ready, take out of the oven and remove the baking beans and greaseproof paper.

Melt half the butter or margarine in a frying pan and gently cook the chopped onion until it is soft and transparent, but not browned, then remove from the heat. Melt the rest of the butter or margarine in a saucepan, then add the grated nutmeg, allow to infuse in the hot fat for 30 seconds then stir in the flour. Gradually whisk in the milk, a little at a time, until the sauce boils and thickens. Reduce to a gentle simmer and cook for a further 3-5 minutes. Add the onions and half the cheese and continue to cook, stirring occasionally, until the cheese has melted, then season to taste. Divide the sauce between the pastry cases. Sprinkle with a mixture of the remaining cheese and breadcrumbs, and place under a moderate grill for a few minutes until the topping is golden and the cheese has melted, taking care not to let the pastry edges burn. Leave to cool for a few minutes before eating – they should be eaten warm, not piping hot.

DOCK PUDDING

The Calder Valley of Yorkshire is famous for its Dock Pudding, which is fried in bacon fat and eaten for breakfast or supper. The plant used is not the common dock, however, but bistort, or sweet dock, which is similar to spinach. It grows in the early spring, and so in former years it was a useful food plant as it provided some fresh greens during the time of the year known as the 'hungry gap', when winter food stores were running out and not much else was yet ready to harvest. A traditional Dock Pudding also contained nettles, wild garlic and oatmeal. The tradition is remembered in the World Dock Pudding Championships which are held every April or May in Mytholmroyd in the Calder Valley.

FACT BOX

The Buttertubs Pass near Thwaite takes its name from the Buttertubs, a number of deep, circular fissures or pot holes in the limestone which were caused by water erosion, and which are said to resemble the wooden tubs in which butter used to be stored.

THWAITE, VILLAGE AND BUTTERTUBS PASS c1960 T135012

RICHMOND, THE CASTLE KEEP 1908 59493

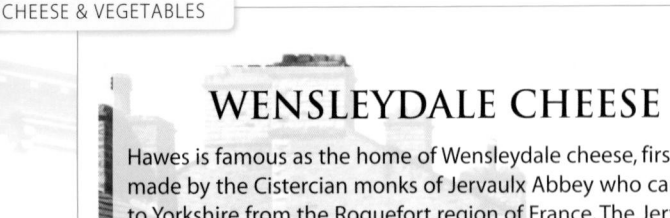

WENSLEYDALE CHEESE

Hawes is famous as the home of Wensleydale cheese, first made by the Cistercian monks of Jervaulx Abbey who came to Yorkshire from the Roquefort region of France. The Jervaulx monks used sheep's milk to make the original Wensleydale cheese, but cow's milk began to be used from the 1300s. In more recent years this delicious cheese has become famous as a favourite of the Wallace character in the 'Wallace and Gromit' animated films, and the Wensleydale Creamery at Hawes now produces a special brand of 'Wallace and Gromit Wensleydale'.

HAWES, MARKET PLACE 1924 75755

RECIPE

WEST RIDING PUDDING

It was the Viking Danes who settled in Yorkshire in the Dark Ages who first divided the huge county into the three Ridings, or 'thridings' (thirds), and they became the North, East and West Ridings before these administrative areas were abolished under the local government reorganisation of 1974.

> 175g/6oz shortcrust pastry
> 2 tablespoonfuls of raspberry jam
> 115g/4oz butter
> 115g/4oz caster sugar
> 2 eggs, beaten
> 115g/4oz self-raising flour
> 25g/1oz ground almonds
> Grated zest of half a lemon

Pre-heat the oven to 180°C/350°F/Gas Mark 4.

Roll out the pastry on a lightly floured surface, and use it to line a greased 20cm (8 inch) pie tin. Spread the base of the tart with raspberry jam.

Cream the butter and sugar together in a bowl until the mixture is light and fluffy. Beat in the eggs a little at a time, adding a little flour if necessary to prevent curdling. Sift the flour into the mixture, then add the ground almonds and grated lemon zest, and gently fold it all in. Turn the mixture into the pie tin and spread it over the jam. Bake in the pre-heated oven for 25-30 minutes, until the filling is well risen and firm and the pastry is golden and crisp.

RECIPE

YORKSHIRE APPLE AND HONEY PUDDING

115g/4oz butter or margarine
115g/4oz caster sugar
115g/4oz plain flour
2 eggs, beaten
50g/2oz soft brown sugar
2 cooking apples
115g/4oz runny honey
A pinch of grated nutmeg
A pinch of salt

Cream the butter and sugar until it is fluffy, then beat in the eggs a little at a time, adding a small amount of flour if necessary to prevent the mixture from curdling. Sift the flour and a pinch of salt into the bowl, and gently fold in until it is all mixed in. Grease a pudding basin and sprinkle the brown sugar over the bottom and around the sides of the dish. Peel, core and slice the apples and put them in the bottom of the basin, then sprinkle the grated nutmeg and dribble the honey over the apple slices. Pour the creamed mixture into the basin and gently spread the surface to cover the apple.

Cover the basin with its lid or a piece of pleated greaseproof paper, tied down securely. Half fill a large saucepan with water, bring to the boil and place the pudding basin inside the saucepan. Replace the lid and steam for 1½ - 2 hours. Check the pan regularly and replenish with more boiling water when necessary, making sure that it does not boil dry.

When the pudding is cooked, turn out from the basin into a serving dish and serve with cream or custard, and a little warmed honey if liked.

This can be cooked in a pressure cooker if preferred, for 45 minutes. It can also be cooked in a microwave oven: use a microwave-safe bowl, and cook on high for 4-5 minutes. To make sure that it is cooked all the way through, wait 2 minutes, then plunge a thin blade into the centre of the pudding. If it has some batter sticking to it, put the pudding back in the oven and microwave for 1 minute longer.

RECIPE

BILBERRY PIE

Bilberries (wild blueberries) can be found on the Yorkshire moors throughout late summer. They grow on small bushes close to the ground and are hard work to pick, but are well worth the effort. However, commercially grown blueberries from the greengrocer or supermarket can be used in this recipe instead. In some parts of Yorkshire in the past, it was traditional to serve Bilberry Pie at a funeral tea.

> 450g/1 lb bilberries (or blueberries)
> 2 cooking apples
> 225g/8oz sugar
> 1 egg, beaten
> 350g/12oz sweet shortcrust or puff pastry, whichever is preferred

Heat the oven to 200°C/400°F/Gas Mark 6.

Remove the cores from the apples with an apple corer, but do not peel them. Stand the apples in an ovenproof dish, add 2 tablespoonfuls of water to the dish and bake in the pre-heated oven for 40-45 minutes, until the apples are tender. When cooked, scrape out the pulp from the apples and mix it with the bilberries and the sugar.

Roll out half the pastry on a lightly floured board and use it to line a greased 20cm (8 inch) pie tin. Turn out the fruit mixture into the pie tin. Roll out the remaining pastry to make a lid and place it over the pie, and trim and seal the edges.

Brush the lid of the pie with beaten egg white and sprinkle with sugar. Place in the pre-heated oven and bake for ten minutes, then reduce the heat to 180°/350°C/Gas Mark 4 and cook for a further 30 minutes until the pastry is golden brown and crisp.

RECITE

YORKSHIRE CURD TART

The distinguishing and traditional characteristic of Yorkshire Curd Tart is allspice (or 'clove pepper' as it was also known) but this may not be to modern tastes, so mixed spice can be substituted for the ground allspice if preferred. In many parts of Yorkshire in the past, it was the custom to offer curd tart to visitors at Whitsuntide in May.

For the pastry:
115g/4oz butter, diced
225g/8oz plain flour
1 egg yolk

For the filling:
A large pinch of ground allspice, or mixed spice if preferred
90g/3½ oz sugar
3 eggs, beaten
Grated rind and juice of 1 lemon
40g/1½ oz melted butter
450g/1 lb curd cheese, or cottage cheese if curd cheese is hard to find
75g/3oz raisins or sultanas

Pre-heat the oven to 190°C/375°F/Gas Mark 5.

To make the pastry: rub the butter into the flour until the mixture resembles fine breadcrumbs. Stir the egg yolk into the flour mixture with a little water to bind the dough together. Turn the dough on to a lightly floured surface, knead lightly and form into a ball. Roll out the pastry thinly and use to line a 20cm (8 inch) fluted loose-bottomed flan tin. Chill for 15 minutes.

To make the filling: mix the ground allspice or mixed spice with the sugar, then stir in the eggs, lemon rind and juice, melted butter, curd or cottage cheese and dried fruit. Pour the filling into the chilled pastry case, then bake in the pre-heated oven for about 40 minutes until the pastry is cooked and the filling is lightly set and golden brown. Serve still slightly warm, cut into wedges with cream.

YORKSHIRE'S RHUBARB TRIANGLE

Most of the rhubarb sold in the UK is produced in Yorkshire, in an area that has become known as 'The Rhubarb Triangle'. Nowadays this is the area between Wakefield, Morley and Rothwell, but in former times it encompassed a much larger area between Wakefield, Leeds and Bradford. Wakefield celebrates its connection with this vegetable that is used like a fruit with an annual Rhubarb Festival in February, and also with a sculpture depicting a rhubarb plant which stands in Holmfield Park in the city. The leaves of the rhubarb plant are highly poisonous, and only the stems are eaten, cooked by poaching or stewing, with sugar added to taste. Tender pink stems of early forced rhubarb, available from January to early April, are a spring treat with a delicate flavour, and do not require peeling before use – just trim off the root ends and the leaves, and cut the rhubarb stalks into small pieces before cooking. Main crop rhubarb is somewhat coarser with its thick stems, stronger colour and more acidic flavour, and tough strings of skin must be peeled off before the stalks are cut into small pieces and cooked. Maincrop rhubarb is in season from mid March to the end of June. Rhubarb is ideal for making pie and crumble fillings, fools, jams and chutneys, and blends well with other flavours, such as orange, cinnamon and ginger – rhubarb and ginger jam makes an interesting alternative to marmalade to spread on your breakfast toast.

**WAKEFIELD, CROSS SQUARE
c1955** W464019

RECITE

RECIPE

RHUBARB CRUMBLE

900g/2 lbs rhubarb stems
225g/8oz caster sugar or light muscovado sugar
The juice and grated zest of one orange
225g/8oz plain flour
115g/4oz butter

Pre-heat the oven to 200°C/400°F/Gas Mark 6.

Trim the rhubarb stalks, peel off the coarse skin if necessary, and chop them up into short lengths about 3cm (1½ inch) long. Put the rhubarb in a wide pan with 115g (4oz) of the sugar, the orange juice and zest and about 4 tablespoons of water. Bring the water to a gentle simmer, and shake the pan a little. The juice will start to come out of the rhubarb at this stage. Leave to bubble gently in the juice for 2-3 minutes, then turn the stems over in the pan so that the top pieces get into the juice, allow to cook for a couple more minutes, then put a lid on the pan, take off the heat and put aside to allow the rhubarb to continue stewing gently in its own juice whilst you make the crumble topping. If you cook it for too long it will go mushy – you want it to stay in chunks.

Mix the flour and the rest of the sugar in a bowl, then add the butter, cut into small pieces, and use your fingertips to rub the butter into the flour and sugar until the mixture resembles breadcrumbs (or do this in a food processor if preferred). Spoon the rhubarb into a shallow baking dish or tin, but only add enough of the juice to half fill the dish, as more juice will come out of the rhubarb as it cooks in the oven. Cover with the crumble mixture and bake in the pre-heated oven for 25-30 minutes, until the crumble topping is crisp and golden. Serve with cream or custard.

HAWES, HAYMAKING 1924 75754

RECIPE

SCARBOROUGH MUFFINS

Muffins are rather like crumpets, but can also be used like toast, topped with a fried egg etc for breakfast, or split and spread with butter. There are different versions of crumpets, pikelets and muffins around the country, but Scarborough muffins are light, soft and fluffy.

350g/12oz plain flour
300ml/½ pint milk
15g/½oz fresh yeast, or ½ tablespoonful dried yeast
1 teaspoonful of sugar
1 egg
A pinch of salt

Warm the milk and stir in the yeast and sugar, then leave for ten minutes until the yeast has activated. Beat the egg and add to the milk. Mix the salt into the flour in a large bow, then work in the milk and egg mixture, making a stiff dough.

Roll out the dough lightly on a floured surface, and cut it into round cakes. Cover them and leave them to rise in a warm place for 30 minutes, than bake them on a baking sheet for 30 minutes in a pre-heated hot oven – 230°C/450°F/Gas Mark 8; turn the muffins halfway through cooking.

Serve the muffins hot, cut in half and spread with butter.

LAND OF GREEN GINGER

At the bottom of Whitefriargate in the centre of Hull Old Town is one of the most intriguingly-named streets in England – Land of Green Ginger. It was formerly known as Old Beverley Street. There are several theories as to how the street got this name, but John Markwell in 'Streets of Hull' explains that this was the part of town where green, or unripe, ginger used to be stored.

HULL, WHITEFRIARGATE 1903 49817

RECIPE

GINGERBREAD

This version of a soft, sponge-like gingerbread comes from the old West Riding area of Yorkshire. It uses golden syrup, which became available towards the end of the 19th century, although black treacle would have been used before that date, and can still be used if preferred.

> 450g/1 lb plain flour
> A pinch of salt
> 2 rounded teaspoonfuls of ground ginger
> 225g/8oz caster sugar, or light soft brown sugar
> 175g/6oz butter or margarine
> 225g/8oz golden syrup (this is about half a 454g tin)
> 1 egg, beaten
> 1 teaspoonful bicarbonate of soda
> A little milk to mix

Pre-heat the oven to 180°C/350°F/Gas mark 4.

Grease a 20-22cm (8-9 inch) baking tin. Sift the flour, salt and ginger into a mixing basin, and stir in the sugar. Melt the butter or margarine and golden syrup in a pan over a gentle heat until the fat has melted, then stir it into the dry ingredients. Allow to cool for a few minutes then stir in the beaten egg. Dissolve the bicarbonate of soda in a little milk and stir into the mixture. Mix it all well together, adding a little more milk if necessary to make a thick batter. Spread the mixture in the greased baking tin and bake in the pre-heated oven for 35-45 minutes, until the top is risen but is still springy to the touch. Leave to cool in the tin, then cut the gingerbread into squares.

RECIPE

YORKSHIRE CHEESECAKE TARTS

These small cheesecake tarts were often served on Yorkshire farms in the past at sheep-shearing time.

For the pastry:
115g/4oz butter or
  margarine
225g/8oz plain flour
1 tablespoonful caster sugar
Pinch of salt
1 egg yolk
1-2 tablespoons cold water

For the filling:
225g/8oz fresh curd or cottage
  cheese, sieved
50g/2oz caster sugar
1 teaspoonful grated lemon rind
2 eggs, separated
2 tablespoonfuls currants or
  sultanas
1 tablespoonful melted butter
Pinch of nutmeg

Make the pastry by rubbing the fat into the flour, adding the sugar, salt and egg yolk, and mixing well. Finally add the cold water to make a firm dough. Turn out on to a floured surface and knead well, then roll into a ball and chill for at least 30 minutes.

Pre-heat the oven to 220°C/425°F/Gas Mark 7.

Mix together all the remaining ingredients except the egg whites. Roll out the pastry. Line 12 greased deep patty tins with the pastry, and lightly prick over the bottoms with a fork.

Beat the egg whites until stiff, and lightly fold into the cheese mixture. Divide the mixture between the patty tin cases, and cook in the pre-heated oven for 10 minutes, then reduce the oven temperature to 180°C/350°F/Gas Mark 4, and continue cooking for a further 20-25 minutes or until the cheese mixture is set and golden.

RECIPE

YORKSHIRE FAT RASCALS

These delicious fruited teacakes with a rich crust are a sort of cross between scones and rock cakes, and are a favourite delicacy in many a Yorkshire tearoom. The original versions would have been cooked in Yorkshire homes either on a 'backstone' or on a griddle over a turf fire, and they were also known as turf cakes in the past. The use of glacé cherries and candied peel is a more recent addition. This quantity should make 8 Fat Rascals.

> 225g/8oz self-raising flour
> 115g/4oz butter or margarine, cut into small pieces
> 75g/3oz caster sugar or light soft brown sugar
> Pinch of salt
> 50g/2oz mixed dried fruit – currants, raisins, sultanas
> 25g/1oz glacé cherries, cut in half
> 25g/1oz chopped candied mixed peel
> 1 egg
> 3-4 tablespoonfuls of milk

Pre-heat the oven to 200°C/400°F/Gas Mark 6, grease 2 baking sheets and line them with baking parchment or greaseproof paper.

Sift the flour into a mixing bowl, add the cubed fat and use your fingertips to rub it into the flour until the mixture resembles fine breadcrumbs (or prepare in a food processor if preferred). Add the sugar, salt, dried fruit, cherries and peel, and mix well. Beat the egg and stir it into the mixture, adding just enough milk to form the mixture into a firm ball of dough – it should not be too wet and sticky.

Lightly flour your hands, and divide the dough into 8 pieces, rolling each piece very lightly between your hands to form it into a ball. Arrange the balls of dough on the prepared baking sheets, dust them with a little caster sugar and bake in the pre-heated oven for about 15-20 minutes, until they are risen and golden brown but before the dried fruit starts to burn. They can be eaten warm from the oven or cold, either just as they are or spread with butter.

FACTBOX

In many parts of Yorkshire it was traditional to make a 'Pepper Cake' at Christmas, which was flavoured with black treacle and allspice, or clove pepper as it was known locally. Pepper Cake was served with a piece of cheese to visitors such as carol singers, and was the subject of a seasonal rhyme sung by children:

'A little bit of pepper cake,
A little bit of cheese,
A little drink of water,
And a penny, if you please!'

ALDBOROUGH, CHILDREN AND CART 1907 58636x

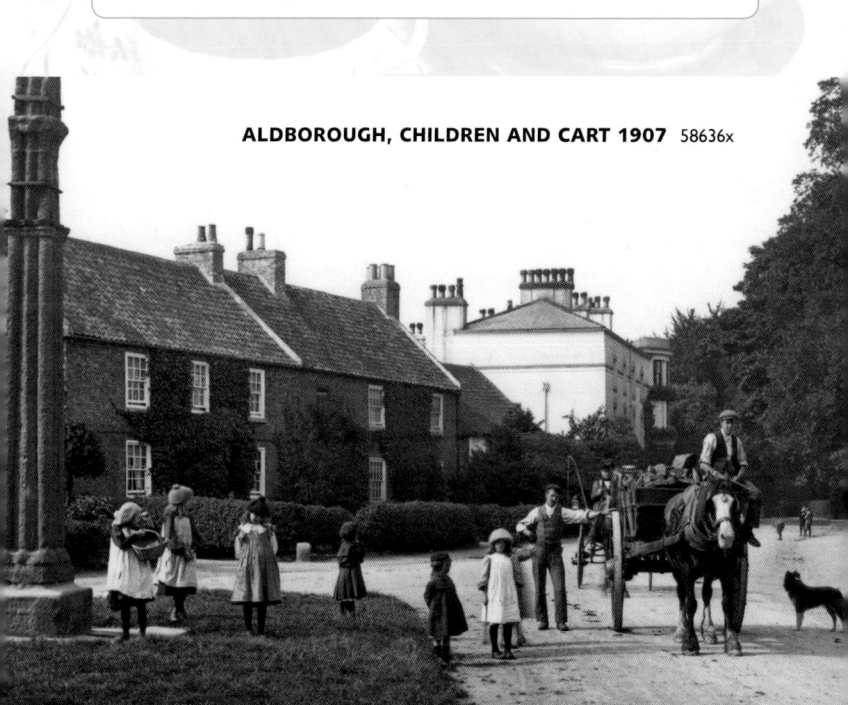

RECIPE

WILFRA TARTS

These delicious small, sweet tarts were traditionally made in Ripon during Wilfra Week in August, a festival commemorating St Wilfrid, the patron saint of Ripon Cathedral. It was the custom during Wilfra Week for local women to make these tarts and leave them on dishes outside their houses, so that passers by could help themselves.

225g/8oz shortcrust pastry
300ml/ ½ pint of milk
25g/1oz fresh white breadcrumbs
115g/4oz butter
50g/2oz ground almonds
3 eggs, beaten
25g/1oz caster sugar
Grated zest of 1 lemon

Pre-heat the oven to 180°C/350°F/Gas Mark 4.

Bring the milk to the boil in a saucepan, and pour it over the breadcrumbs in a mixing bowl. Stir, and leave for 10 minutes for the breadcrumbs to absorb the milk.

Grease a tray of patty tins. Roll out the pastry on a lightly floured surface, and use it to line the patty tins.

Cut the butter into small pieces and add to the milk and breadcrumbs. Stir in until the butter has melted. Add the ground almonds, sugar and grated lemon zest. Beat in the eggs, a little at a time. Fill the pastry cases in the patty tins with the mixture, and bake in the pre-heated oven for about 20-25 minutes until the filling is risen and set.

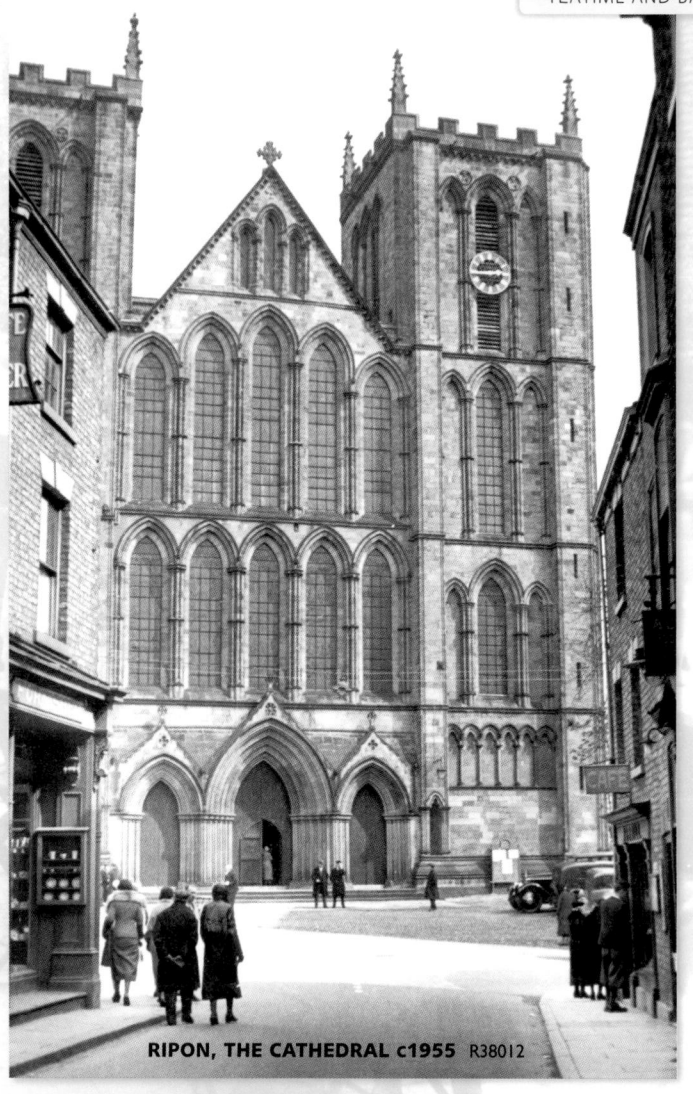

RIPON, THE CATHEDRAL c1955 R38012

RECIPE

SLY CAKE

This pastry slice gets its name because its plain appearance hides a deceptively rich filling of dried fruit and nuts. Either dates or dried figs can be used, as preferred.

For the rich shortcrust pastry:
225g/8oz plain flour
50g/2oz margarine or butter
50g/2oz lard
25g/1oz caster sugar
1 beaten egg
Make the pastry in the usual way adding the sugar and egg after rubbing in the fat, and before adding a little water to form the pastry dough

For the filling:
175g/6oz dates or dried figs, stoned and chopped into pieces
50g/2oz currants
50g/2oz raisins
50g/2oz chopped walnuts
50g/2oz dark soft brown sugar
Grated rind of half a lemon
6 tablespoonfuls of water
Milk to glaze
Caster sugar for dusting

Put the dates or figs, dried fruit, walnuts, sugar, lemon rind and water into a pan and cook very gently over a low heat, stirring occasionally to make sure it does not stick and burn, until the fruit has absorbed the liquid and the mixture is soft. Put aside to cool for a few minutes.

Pre-heat the oven to 190°C/375°F/Gas Mark 5 and grease a shallow baking tin about 20-22cm (8-9 inches) square. Divide the pastry dough into two pieces, roll out one piece on a lightly floured surface and use it to line the base and sides of the baking tin. Spread the fruit mixture evenly over the dough. Brush round the pastry edge with a little milk. Roll out the other piece of dough and use it to cover the filling. Seal the pastry edges well together, and brush the top of the cake with a little milk. Bake in the pre-heated oven for about 30 minutes, until the pastry is golden. Remove from the oven, sprinkle the top with caster sugar, and leave to cool in the tin. When cool, cut it into 12 squares.

RECITE

RECIPE

PARKIN

In some parts of Yorkshire it was traditional to eat parkin on Bonfire Night, 5th November. The black treacle gives this the true dark parkin colour.

> 300ml/ ½ pint milk
> 225g/8oz golden syrup
> 225g/8oz black treacle
> 115g/4oz butter or margarine
> 50g/2oz dark brown sugar
> 450g/1 lb plain flour
> Half a teaspoonful of bicarbonate of soda
> 1½ teaspoonfuls of ground ginger
> 350g/12oz medium oatmeal
> 1 egg, beaten

Pre-heat the oven to 180°C/350°F/Gas Mark 4.

Put the milk, syrup, treacle, butter or margarine and sugar into a saucepan and heat gently, stirring all the time, until the mixture has melted and is smooth. Take care not to let the mixture boil. When it has mixed together, take it off the heat and leave to cool for a few minutes.

Put the flour, bicarbonate of soda, ginger and oatmeal into a large bowl and mix together. Make a well in the centre, pour in the beaten egg, then gradually pour in the milk and syrup mixture, stirring all the time, until it has formed a smooth batter.

Grease a 20cm (8 inch) square cake tin, and line the bottom with greaseproof paper. Pour the batter into the tin. Bake in the pre-heated oven for about 45 minutes, until the surface of the parkin is firm to the touch.

Allow the parkin to cool in the tin for a few minutes, then turn out on to a wire rack to cool completely. Cut into pieces when cool, and store in an airtight tin, preferably for 3 days, before eating.

RECIPE

APPLE FRITTERS

Apple fritters used to be a traditional treat in many parts of Yorkshire for Ash Wednesday, the first day of Lent and 46 days before Easter in the Christian religious calendar.

> 225g/8oz flour
> 3 eggs
> 300ml/ ½ pint of milk
> 225g/8oz currants
> 4 cooking apples
> Lard or oil for frying
> Caster or icing sugar for dredging.

Sift the flour into a large mixing bowl and make a well in the centre. Break the eggs into the well, and beat them into the flour, drawing the flour in from the sides, until it has all mixed together thoroughly into a smooth paste. Gradually add the milk, a little at a time, beating continually to make a batter.

Pore and core the apples and chop them into small pieces. Mix the apple pieces and the currants into the batter.

Heat the lard or oil in a large pan. Drop in spoonfuls of the batter and fry the fritters until they are crisp and golden. Drain and dry on absorbent kitchen paper, then dredge with sugar and eat whilst still hot.

FACTBOX

Liquorice is known as 'Spanish' in some parts of Yorkshire, and is particularly associated with the town of Pontefract. The Crusaders of the 12th century probably introduced the liquorice plant to Pontefract, and from that grew a hugely important industry; it still flourishes today, but the liquorice roots are no longer grown locally. The disc-shaped sweets flavoured with liquorice known as Pontefract Cakes (or 'Pomfret' or 'Pomfrey' Cakes) are still made in the town, and an annual liquorice festival is held there, where liquorice flavoured cheese, ice-cream and beer can be sampled. Photograph 71339 (below) shows the busy marketplace in Settle in the 1920s. Settle has an ebbing and flowing well, a spring which issues from the limestone as its hits impervious rocks beneath, ebbing and flowing as the water flow dictates, thanks to a natural siphon in the rock, and there used to be a local tradition on Easter Day of mixing the well water with liquorice and drinking it.

SETTLE, MARKET DAY 1921 71339

RECIPE

TREACLE TOFFEE

Bonfire Night on 5th November commemorates the foiled Gunpowder Plot of 1605 to blow up James I and his parliament in London with 36 barrels of gunpowder. Guy Fawkes, who was caught in the cellars of the House of Lords about to set fire to the fuse which would set off the explosion, was born in York in 1570. Treacle Toffee is traditionally eaten in Yorkshire on Bonfire Night. In some places it is made twisted into long lengths and known as Tom Trot Toffee.

450g/1 lb soft brown sugar
5 tablespoonfuls of water
2 teaspoonfuls of vinegar
25g/1oz butter
150ml/ ¼ pint black treacle

Put the sugar into a saucepan with the water and vinegar and when dissolved add the butter and the treacle. Heat gently until the butter and treacle melt. Raise the heat and boil for 12-15 minutes. The temperature can be checked with a sugar thermometer, and should reach around 140°C (280°F).

Pour the treacle into a greased or oiled tin and leave until partially set. Score the toffee with a knife into bars or squares, and when cold break up and store in an airtight tin.

YORK, GOODRAMGATE 1892 30631

YORKSHIRE TOFFEE

Halifax is often known as 'Toffee Town'. It was here that John Mackintosh invented his famous toffee in the 1890s, a cross between traditional English toffee which was rock hard and American toffee in the soft caramel style. He and his wife first sold the toffee from their pastry shop at King Cross. John Mackintosh's company merged with Rowntree of York in 1988, but his most famous creation is still popular – Quality Street.

HALIFAX, SOUTHGATE 1896 38774

Another of Yorkshire's toffee towns is Harrogate, famous for Farrah's toffee which is sold in distinctive blue and silver embossed tins. The Farrah's toffee works can be seen on the left of photograph 58648 (opposite). The company was established in 1840 by John Farrah, and Farrah's Toffee was originally produced to counteract the unpleasant sulphurous taste of the mineral water that made Harrogate into one of the country's premier spa towns in the past – the water was efficacious in the treatment of internal parasites like worms which afflicted much of the country's population in former centuries.

HARROGATE, CRESCENT GARDENS
1907 58648

Flavours of ...
YORKSHIRE
SWEETS AND TREATS

CENTRAL
GARAGE

FRANCIS FRITH

PIONEER VICTORIAN PHOTOGRAPHER

Francis Frith, founder of the world-famous photographic archive, was a complex and multi-talented man. A devout Quaker and a highly successful Victorian businessman, he was philosophical by nature and pioneering in outlook. By 1855 he had already established a wholesale grocery business in Liverpool, and sold it for the astonishing sum of £200,000, which is the equivalent today of over £15,000,000. Now in his thirties, and captivated by the new science of photography, Frith set out on a series of pioneering journeys up the Nile and to the Near East.

INTRIGUE AND EXPLORATION

He was the first photographer to venture beyond the sixth cataract of the Nile. Africa was still the mysterious 'Dark Continent', and Stanley and Livingstone's historic meeting was a decade into the future. The conditions for picture taking confound belief. He laboured for hours in his wicker dark-room in the sweltering heat of the desert, while the volatile chemicals fizzed dangerously in their trays. Back in London he exhibited his photographs and was 'rapturously cheered' by members of the Royal Society. His reputation as a photographer was made overnight.

VENTURE OF A LIFE-TIME

By the 1870s the railways had threaded their way across the country, and Bank Holidays and half-day Saturdays had been made obligatory by Act of Parliament. All of a sudden the working man and his family were able to enjoy days out, take holidays, and see a little more of the world.

With typical business acumen, Francis Frith foresaw that these new tourists would enjoy having souvenirs to commemorate their days out. For the next thirty years he travelled the country by train and by pony and trap, producing fine photographs of seaside resorts and beauty spots that were keenly bought by millions of Victorians. These prints were painstakingly pasted into family albums and pored over during the dark nights of winter, rekindling precious memories of summer excursions. Frith's studio was soon supplying retail shops all over the country, and by 1890 F Frith & Co had become the greatest specialist photographic publishing company in the world, with over 2,000 sales outlets, and pioneered the picture postcard.

FRANCIS FRITH'S LEGACY

Francis Frith had died in 1898 at his villa in Cannes, his great project still growing. By 1970 the archive he created contained over a third of a million pictures showing 7,000 British towns and villages.

Frith's legacy to us today is of immense significance and value, for the magnificent archive of evocative photographs he created provides a unique record of change in the cities, towns and villages throughout Britain over a century and more. Frith and his fellow studio photographers revisited locations many times down the years to update their views, compiling for us an enthralling and colourful pageant of British life and character.

We are fortunate that Frith was dedicated to recording the minutiae of everyday life. For it is this sheer wealth of visual data, the painstaking chronicle of changes in dress, transport, street layouts, buildings, housing and landscape that captivates us so much today, offering us a powerful link with the past and with the lives of our ancestors.

Computers have now made it possible for Frith's many thousands of images to be accessed almost instantly. The archive offers every one of us an opportunity to examine the places where we and our families have lived and worked down the years. Its images, depicting our shared past, are now bringing pleasure and enlightenment to millions around the world a century and more after his death.

For further information visit: www.francisfrith.com

INTERIOR DECORATION

Frith's photographs can be seen framed and as giant wall murals in thousands of pubs, restaurants, hotels, banks, retail stores and other public buildings throughout Britain. These provide interesting and attractive décor, generating strong local interest and acting as a powerful reminder of gentler days in our increasingly busy and frenetic world.

FRITH PRODUCTS

All Frith photographs are available as prints and posters in a variety of different sizes and styles. In the UK we also offer a range of other gift and stationery products illustrated with Frith photographs, although many of these are not available for delivery outside the UK – see our web site for more information on the products available for delivery in your country.

THE INTERNET

Over 100,000 photographs of Britain can be viewed and purchased on the Frith web site. The web site also includes memories and reminiscences contributed by our customers, who have personal knowledge of localities and of the people and properties depicted in Frith photographs. If you wish to learn more about a specific town or village you may find these reminiscences fascinating to browse. Why not add your own comments if you think they would be of interest to others? See **www.francisfrith.com**

PLEASE HELP US BRING FRITH'S PHOTOGRAPHS TO LIFE

Our authors do their best to recount the history of the places they write about. They give insights into how particular towns and villages developed, they describe the architecture of streets and buildings, and they discuss the lives of famous people who lived there. But however knowledgeable our authors are, the story they tell is necessarily incomplete.

Frith's photographs are so much more than plain historical documents. They are living proofs of the flow of human life down the generations. They show real people at real moments in history; and each of those people is the son or daughter of someone, the brother or sister, aunt or uncle, grandfather or grandmother of someone else. All of them lived, worked and played in the streets depicted in Frith's photographs.

We would be grateful if you would give us your insights into the places shown in our photographs: the streets and buildings, the shops, businesses and industries. Post your memories of life in those streets on the Frith website: what it was like growing up there, who ran the local shop and what shopping was like years ago; if your workplace is shown tell us about your working day and what the building is used for now. Read other visitors' memories and reconnect with your shared local history and heritage. With your help more and more Frith photographs can be brought to life, and vital memories preserved for posterity, and for the benefit of historians in the future.

Wherever possible, we will try to include some of your comments in future editions of our books. Moreover, if you spot errors in dates, titles or other facts, please let us know, because our archive records are not always completely accurate—they rely on 140 years of human endeavour and hand-compiled records. You can email us using the contact form on the website.

Thank you!

For further information, trade, or author enquiries
please contact us at the address below:

The Francis Frith Collection, Unit 6, Oakley Business Park, Wylye Road, Dinton, Wiltshire SP3 5EU.
Tel: +44 (0)1722 716 376 Fax: +44 (0)1722 716 881
e-mail: sales@francisfrith.co.uk **www.francisfrith.com**